SAFETY ON WHEELS

SAFETY FIRST

Written by
Susan Kesselring

Illustrated by
Dan McGeehan

www.av2books.com

Go to **www.av2books.com,** and enter this book's unique code.

BOOK CODE

AVZ98686

AV² by Weigl brings you media enhanced books that support active learning.

AV² provides enriched content that supplements and complements this book. Weigl's AV² books strive to create inspired learning and engage young minds in a total learning experience.

Your AV² Media Enhanced books come alive with...

Audio
Listen to sections of the book read aloud.

Video
Watch informative video clips.

Embedded Weblinks
Gain additional information for research.

Try This!
Complete activities and hands-on experiments.

Key Words
Study vocabulary, and complete a matching word activity.

Quizzes
Test your knowledge.

Slide Show
View images and captions, and prepare a presentation.

... and much, much more!

Published by AV² by Weigl
350 5th Avenue, 59th Floor New York, NY 10118
Website: www.av2books.com

Library of Congress Cataloging-in-Publication Data

Names: Kesselring, Susan, auhtor.
Title: Safety on wheels / Susan Kesselring.
Description: New York, NY : AV² by Weigl, 2020. | Series: Safety first | Audience: K to Grade 3.
Identifiers: LCCN 2018053407 (print) | LCCN 2018054536 (ebook) | ISBN 9781489699732 (Multi User Ebook) | ISBN 9781489699749 (Single User Ebook) | ISBN 9781489699718 (hardcover : alk. paper) | ISBN 9781489699725 (softcover : alk. paper)
Subjects: LCSH: Cycling--Safety measures--Juvenile literature. | Skateboarding--Safety measures--Juvenile literature. | In-line skating--Safety measures--Juvenile literature.
Classification: LCC GV1055 (ebook) | LCC GV1055 .K47 2020 (print) | DDC 796.6028/9--dc23
LC record available at https://lccn.loc.gov/2018053407

Printed in the United States of America in Brainerd, Minnesota
1 2 3 4 5 6 7 8 9 0 22 21 20 19 18

112018
102918

Project Coordinator: Jared Siemens Designer: Ana María Vidal

First published by The Child's World in 2011

In this book, you will learn about

wheel sport safety,

what to do,

what not to do,

and much more!

How do you like to ride? Is in-line skating your thing? Do you zoom down the street on your bike? Or do you like riding ramps and doing tricks on your skateboard?

Rolling on wheels is tons of fun. But you can get hurt if you are not careful. That is why you should learn how to be safe on your favorite wheels!

Before you ride a bike, you need to make sure it fits you. Check out the bike's seat height. It should be high enough that your knees bend slightly when the pedals are closest to the ground. Next, look at the handlebars. They should be as high as the seat. Lastly, sit on your bike and make sure you can place your feet flat on the ground.

Keep your music player off while on wheels. Headphones can keep you from hearing cars coming your way.

Whatever wheels you ride, be sure to wear the right safety gear. Always wear a helmet. It can save your life if you fall hard.

Your helmet should fit snugly on your head. The front of the helmet should sit about 1 inch (2.5 centimeters) above your eyebrows. Only one or two fingers should fit between the strap and your chin.

In some states, it's the law to wear a helmet.

Next step, pads. On a scooter, wear elbow and knee pads. Add wrist guards for skateboarding and in-line skating. Pads can keep you from breaking bones and getting major cuts if you crash.

When using your bike, skateboard, or scooter, wear shoes that stay on your feet. Tie your laces tight so they don't get caught in the pedals or wheels.

It is not a good idea to ride your wheels at night. It is hard to see where you are going in the dark. Cars can't see you very well, either.

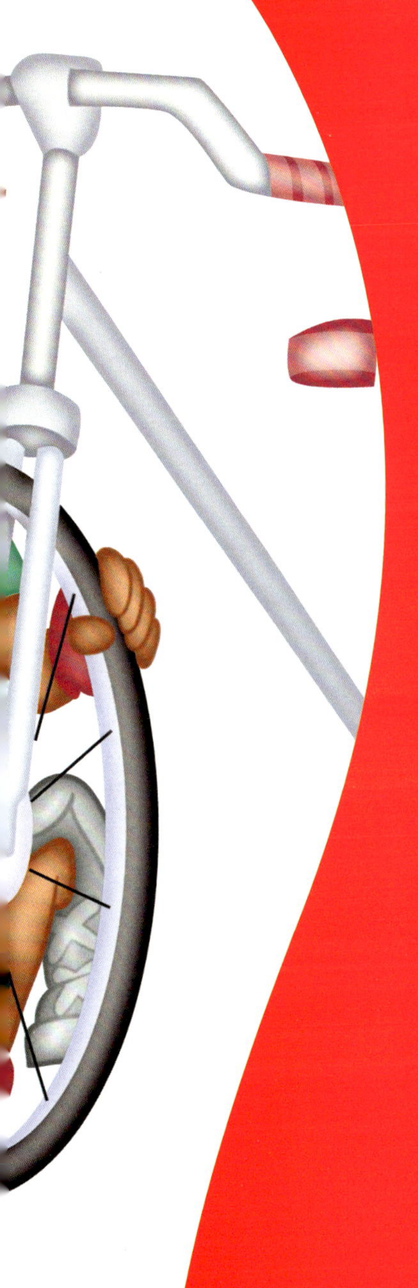

Great! You've got your safety gear on. Now it's time to check a few things. Try the brakes on your bike or scooter to make sure they work. Feel the tires. They should be full of air.

Check your wheels to make sure they're free of sticks, rocks, and other things. Now you're ready to roll!

No matter what kind of wheels you ride, stay on the pavement. Avoid dirt, gravel, and potholes. If you hit a bump, you could lose your balance and crash. Avoid wheeling through water. It could be slippery.

Most wheels are built for one person to ride. Don't let friends ride your bike, skateboard, or scooter with you.

On a bike and a scooter, it's best to always keep both hands on the handlebars. You might have to quickly steer away from something. It's easier to do this when using both hands.

Ride away from the road. Focus on the path in front of you as you ride. If you need to carry anything, put it in a backpack or bike basket. That way, your hands are able to steer the bike.

The part of the skateboard the rider stands on is called the deck. It's made of wood, plastic, or aluminum.

Riding a skateboard is cool, too! Be sure to ask an adult to watch. Try out a skate park. They are great places to ride!

If you want to learn skateboarding tricks, ask if you can take a skateboarding class. If you can't, that's okay, too. You can learn a trick from a friend or an older sibling. Just make sure an adult is there. You shouldn't try tricks on your own.

Have you been in-line skating? It is a great way to go places. But you need to know how to stop. You don't want to roll into a street or lose control and fall.

In-line skates usually have brakes on the back. To use them, tip one foot up so the brake rubs on the ground. This will slow you down. Practice using the brake until you're good at stopping.

You can go so fast on wheels! Bike around the park, scoot on a bike path, or just skate down the block. However you're rolling, be safe and have fun!

KEY WORDS

Research has shown that as much as 65 percent of all written material published in English is made up of 300 words. These 300 words cannot be taught using pictures or learned by sounding them out. They must be recognized by sight. This book contains 129 common sight words to help young readers improve their reading fluency and comprehension. This book also teaches young readers several important content words, such as proper nouns.

Page	Sight Words First Appearance
4	and, do, down, how, is, like, on, or, the, thing, to, you, your
5	are, be, but, can, for, get, have, I, if, learn, me, not, of, should, tell, that, watch, why, will
7	a, as, at, before, cars, enough, feet, from, high, it, keep, look, make, need, next, off, out, place, they, way, when, while
9	about, above, always, between, hard, head, in, it's, life, one, only, right, some, states, two
11	add, cuts, don't, so
12	good, idea, night, see, very, well, where
13	air, few, got, great, now, other, time, try, work
15	could, kind, let, most, no, through, water, what, with
17	away, both, carry, hands, might, put, something, this
18	made, part
19	an, another, ask, just, own, take, there, too, want
21	back, been, go, into, know, stop, them, until, up, use
23	around, even

Page	Content Words First Appearance
4	bike, in-line skating, ramps, skateboard, tricks
5	wheels
7	ground, handlebars, headphones, knees, music player, pedals, seat
9	chin, eyebrows, fingers, helmet, law, strap
11	bones, elbow, laces, pads, scooter, shoes, wrist guards
12	brakes, rocks, sticks, tires
15	balance, bump, dirt, friends, gravel, pavement, potholes
17	backpack, basket, path, road
18	aluminum, deck, plastic, wood
19	adult, class, skate park, sibling
21	street
23	block, sidewalk

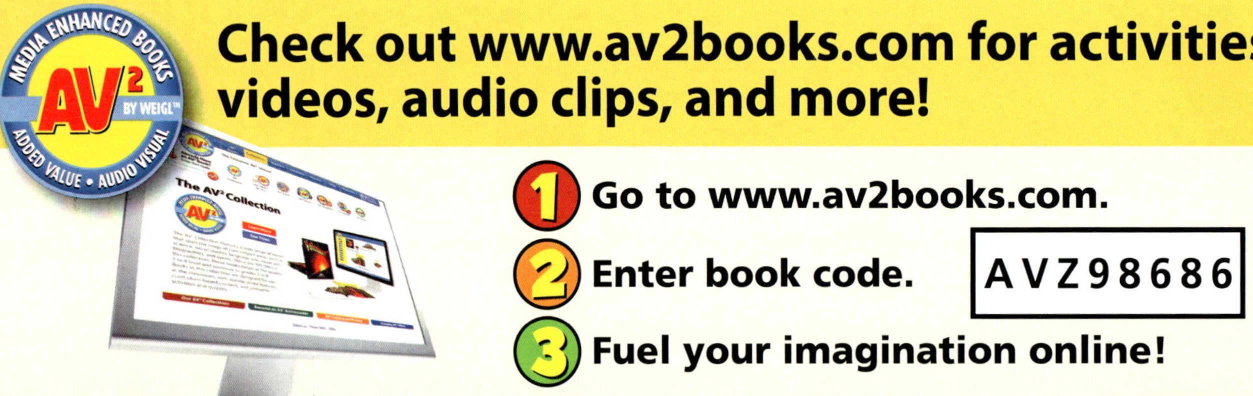

Check out www.av2books.com for activities, videos, audio clips, and more!

1. **Go to www.av2books.com.**
2. **Enter book code.** AVZ98686
3. **Fuel your imagination online!**

www.av2books.com